Joy365

Joy365
Inspirational
Affirmations and Proverbs Book

EPMcKnight, M.Ed.

Words have very powerful meanings and connotations. Once you digest them into your true spirit, your subconscious, they will be life changing, cathartic, and freeing of the mind, soul, body and spirit. Some words have dual meanings and purposes.

Nikaoimani Productions
California

Joy 365

Joy365 Inspirational Affirmations and Proverbs Book

Copyright © 2013 by

Nikao Imani Productions,
POB 4835
West Hills, CA 91308
Published in 2013

ISBN:0-9654807-4-7
Cover designed by Valerie Wade
Editor: Marilyn Zelinsky
www.zazzle.com/valdcreations

CRSDesign.com
Chatsworth, CA

Printed in the United States

Joy 365

OTHER BOOKS:

Words 'N' Action
Catch the Spirit
Lessons of Black History Makers

Plays:

My Daddy's Place
MenApause
The ObamaCare Ward
The Man Who Stands
Ethnically Ambiguous
Trial of Scottsboro Al.

Dedicated to my transitioned Father, Paul
Goldsmith, for my writing ability and my lovely
Mother, Lucille Goldsmith, for wisdom.

Heartfelt appreciation to my beloved family and
friends who have always been supportive with
love and encouragement.

Abandoning

Whatever or whomever is standing between you and a better life, go around it, or over it, or under it, and if you have to, go through it by any means necessary.

Abiding

Your best company is yourself. Make meditative time to dwell with your innermost gut feelings, seeking to unveil your blueprint that you were born with. Abiding with oneself will discover your truth.

Absorbing

Every day is unique with newness for discovery. See it, feel it and act on it with every fiber of your being. Sprint forth with renewed thought, energy and determination. Absorbing that you have the power and the time is now.

Accomplishing

Seek and you shall find. All that you are and need is at your fingertips. Shove negativity out the window and open up the positivity door while removing the blinders from your spirit accomplishing all the beautiful morsels awaiting your grasp.

Acorning

The acorn is in the oak, leave your neighbor's tree alone, go for silence and find your acorn in your oak.

Acting

Think, act, and believe. People who are successful have a tendency to act on their thoughts as opposed to just thinking or talking about them. If you're going to be successful, acting is a quality you must possess whole-heartedly, otherwise someday you find yourself wishing you had.

Adding

Adding years to longevity is a blessing but adding a quality life to your years is priceless.

Advising

Beware of an advisor who directs you down a path never taken or tells you how to succeed and never has.

Aging

Getting older is a blessing and not a curse. While youth may be wasted on the young, aging gives solace to the spirit for having been, seen and done. Wisdom and memories comes with aging and no one can take them away.

A'ing

Awareness, application and appreciation, three a's to change your life. First you must be aware of your plight, what to do and how to do it, then celebrate you for having done it your way, you dare say.

Aiming

Be not afraid to set your sights sky high. Use your mind like a sling shot, close one eye and aim all your vision on the target before you, then release to be assured that you will target and hit the bullseye. Trust, be confident and focus with clear vision aiming toward your goal, don't blink or doubt for a second as you release your bow straight into your target.

<u>Aligning</u>

God will not allow you to walk onto your
dream and have an illegitimate child as long
as you seek guidance in all your decisions
and efforts. Avoid the potholes and pitfalls
of life having an illegitimate child on the
wrong road. Instead, give birth to a full term
healthy bundle of joy on the highway of
success.

<u>Allotting</u>

Always show more kindness than seems
necessary, because the person receiving it
needs it more than you will ever know. As
the old saying goes, "To the world, you may
be one person, but to one person you may be
the world." Allotting is your decree.

Ambushing

Distractions appear in a split second, often slowing down your momentum like a train loaded down with tons of coal tugging along. Ambush them from your subconscious and watch as your caboose picks up speed every time you ambush each distraction, now moving like the bullet train.

Angering

Anger is the thief of patience when you permit. Whatever obstacles come your way, stay calm and allow your spirit to guide you toward peace to circumvent anger from clouding your judgment.

Appearing

Whatever you do, show up and show out. Your appearance will validate the wait.

6

Appearing

No's are the channel to a reservoir of Yes's.
Sail through the tough water, use your
paddle when needed, just don't stop. Be not
disturbed for the next no, it may be the
gateway to the yes hoped for.

Appreciating

Appreciate true love. True love makes the
world look different, problems solvable,
challenges mere distractions, frowns become
smiles, duties are pleasures, commitment is
lovely and togetherness is a joy as the spirit
leaps within you, appreciating every second.

Appreciating

Life is so unpredictable, one minute you're happy, the next moment you're sad. You couldn't appreciate one without experiencing the other. It's a phase and a stage, this too shall pass.

Appreciating

Appreciating what you have is paramount to getting more. Gratitude begets gratitude, like anger attracts anger. The law of attraction gives you what you put out. Embed appreciation in your subconscious and see it unfold when you least expect.

Asking

Ask a question and be a fool for five minutes, don't ask a question and remain a fool for life.

<u>Awakening</u>

Every awakened day, choose to soar as high as possible, discard any negative thoughts, people, situations or energy deflecting your flow. An eagle soars alone and not with a lot of geese. The road to success can be lonely but along the lines you will meet a few others who get your essence.

<u>Backsliding</u>

Taking inventory of your state, your position will not stop you from backsliding because of circumstances but will allow you to be aware of the difference in your life. As you realize that backsliding is okay for the moment it will pass providing you don't give up and at the next junction, make a U-turn.

Baiting

See what you want, decide what bait to use,
dangle it before the prey, move in for the
kill. Back and forth, trial and error, until
baited then reel it in with all your might.

Balancing

Balancing is the key to a life worth living.
With love, work and play, you will
illuminate your sphere, internally and
externally, attracting a quality of life that
feeds not only you but all those that are in
contact with you. You are what you eat.

Balancing

Life is about balance, spiritually, physically, mentally and socially. Even too much of a good thing causes the others to unbalance. Too much exercise can destroy the body without rest, taking in too much water dilutes the body's chemistry, too much reading weakens the eyes, too much socializing catches up with you. In all things get balance.

Banking

Sell your past and open up your future. Your power lies with you. Forget trying to recover defaults of yesterday, but deposit day by day to begin anew.

Bathing

Always begin with a new slate, bathe away
dead cells of thoughts, people and ideas. If
they are difficult to eliminate scrub and
scrub until the old is replaced with the new.
New cells renewed are like putting on a
beautiful fragrance of will do, can do and
shall do. Lotion on love for yourself and
others and enjoy the touch.

Beautying

Age comes, but you don't have to wear it on
your face or body. Exercise, eat healthy,
rest, love, groom and allow your inner
beauty to triumph over the outer which will
not fade.

Befriending

Every person that comes across your path, comes across for a reason and a season. Befriend, get to know, there may be a pot a gold that belies the exterior that you have been waiting for or you may possess the pot of gold they are seeking. All things for a reason and a season, never for naught.

Begging

Never stand begging for that which you have the power to earn. Seek until you have done all you can. Begging should be a need and not your creed. Learn the difference before you proceed.

Beginning

Every day is the first day of the rest of your life, new beginning. Strive to move forward and not struggle with yesterday's setbacks. Reflect, reject, regroup and conquer.

Being

When preaching or teaching the word of
God, remember only use words when it's
absolutely necessary or required.

Being

There is no time like the present to fulfill
your dream. If not now, when, if not you,
who. It's your life, live it. Bloom where you
are planted, enjoy the sunlight as you sprout
outright.

Beneficiaring

Find the beauty, positiveness and joy in
others and become a beneficiary of beauty,
positiveness and joy. Life is a two-way
street. What you give out, you attract.

14

Bettering

When better is possible, then good is never enough. Why settle joining the ranks of many, when being better you set the bar for others to strive.

Bettering

Good is the enemy of better, don't let small thinking keep you inside the black box.

Blessing

Giving to another is a two-fold blessing. What you give comes back to you, perhaps in a different form or source. Having given is divine and receiving later is sweet icing on your cake.

Blowing

Blowing your stack, you have just added to
a polluted world. Refrain, the pollution is
one iota less and we all breathe less
pollution and better.

Boiling

Stuff happens to you, near you, around you
causing the hairs on your neck to rise up like
a lion about to attack, the palms of your
hands now moist, your brow dripping with
perspiration, palpitations of the heart, your
pulse is thumping, you are boiling out of
control. Your soul cries out for solace and
harmony. Meditate until your inner being is
chilled to the bone and boiling resides no
longer, unclouding your soul.

Boiling

When life starts to boil out of control, turn off the heat, check your temperature and uncover the source.

Boosting

Smiling boosts your immune system unlike any meds on the market while frowning breaks it down like poison ivy in your belly.

Breathing

Take a moment, inhale love and exhale bitterness and anger, you're not immune. It grabs you in the gut in a nanosecond, just breathe and release.

Calculating

A new idea, new job, new venture, staying one step ahead of the competition will keep you current and successful. Be abreast of what it takes to move forward and broaden your horizon. You can't build a house without having an idea of the cost from the onset. Calculate the cost, time and energy required, at the end of the day there will be no major surprises or unforeseen setbacks.

Calming

In the midst of the storm, seek to remain calm for in your calmness your answers will appear. Meditate, sit quietly, chant, or just rest, freeing your spirit from clutter to proceed forward with ease, clarity and precision. With earplugs in your ears, you can't hear the siren behind you, likewise clear your spirit to receive internally.

Caring

Humans, like animals, don't care how much you know until you truly and respectfully show them how much you care.

Celebrating

Never a day should pass that isn't celebrated for at least one good thing, even a bad thing. If you don't faint, a bad thing turns out to be a good thing, perhaps a lesson learned, spiritually, naturally or socially. Focus on not what happened to you, but having gone through it and survived evolving to a better you.

Celebrating

Celebrate the good and be thankful,
comprehend the not so good, learn your
lessons and know that it's also good for it
will make or break you, if you allow. In the
end, all trials and triumphs are truly for your
good. If you don't see it today, you will
tomorrow. Like the old folks say, "keep
living."

Challenging

Challenges come to teach us something.
Learn it and you won't repeat it. Today you
may feel challenged because your
refrigerator is not working, until you see
your neighbor's house engulfed in fire. This
challenge could have been your plight, so
see this reality and be grateful for a little
refrigerator challenge.

Challenging

Challenges are mere obstacles while building your mental house. They are the gateway to a solid foundation which no wind can destroy. Brick by brick, a challenging labor, but the house you build will sustain you like a fortress.

Championing

Champion yourself, no matter the circumstances, you don't control all but you do control you.

Changing

The only thing that is constant in life is change, so embrace it and move on.

Changing

No one can change your opinion without your permission. Protect it in a sacred part of your mind as you explore other ideas. Others may seek to devour, arm yourself with mental gear that cannot be penetrated.

Changing

There is a vast difference between having to say something and having something to say. When it comes out it will be validated one way or the other.

Cheerleading

Every team has its cheerleaders and when they score the cheerleaders dance and celebrate and the team's ego builds. Find one cheerleader to celebrate you at all times, building you up like the Eiffel Tower. When you lean to the left or right, like a pilot they steady you as you continue your flight.

<u>Cleaning</u>

Clean out your mental space and free your
spirit. Walk with clarity away from clutter.

<u>Cleaning</u>

Clean your window for a better view and not
because someone demanded you to. The dirt
you see, is the dirt you get.

<u>Clearing</u>

When clouds block your sun, move closer to
God and the nearer you get to Him the
clearer all things will appear.

Clenching

A clenched fist, nothing goes in and nothing comes out, so you keep what you have always had, no more no less.

Clocking

Time waits for no one. Never has and never will. Time is endless there is no beginning and no end. Take stock of how your time is spent. Balance your time between personal and business, for each has its place and will bring much joy when kept in its prospective. Forsake none, and none will forsake you.

Clothing

When clothing yourself in hand-me-downs - ideas, choices or events, find what fits you and work it.

Clothing

Know the company you keep, sheep wear wolves' clothing masquerading down the street of good intentions to unclothe you when you least expect.

Cluttering

Where there is clutter, there is blockage. Where there is blockage, there is hindrance, where there is hindrance there is unfulfillment. Cluttering will impede and affect all that you set your notions to. It's a psychological phenomenon. Decluttering physically and mentally is cathartic. Clutter rivals order and cannot reside together. Order your steps, clear the clutter.

Combating

A momentary setback can be a momentary setup for a long term comeback.

Communing

From the earth we come, back to the earth we go communing. Nature is medicinal, like a duck in water, like going home and feeling at peace, like being where you are supposed to be, like the birds chirping all around, like fresh morning dew gracing your brow, as the winds blow all around you communing. We are one with nature.

Compassing

Keep your eyes on your prize, and not your neighbor's, your compass may falter.

Conceiving

Believe with conviction that you can be anything you want to be, then act steadfastly with your belief. What the mind conceives, the mind will achieve.

26

Confiding

Everyone needs a confidante to cheer them on. Yet we are all human and let each other down, purposely or not but you can be confident about the future, when you walk with God in the present.

Conquering

Some days you feel like you can conquer the world, and you are unstoppable. Then there are those days that you are dragging and wondering what the hell. Take a moment, reflect back to yesterday's conquerings as you propel yourself back on the battlefield to success. You are more than a conqueror for you did it once, you can do it again.

Controlling

Walk the dog, don't let the dog walk you.
That irresistible brownie in your refrigerator,
the cheesecake or the bread consumes and
controls your every thought. You'd better
walk the dog before the dog walks you.

Coping

Close deceiving friends are difficult to cope
with, than out and out enemies in your face.

Coughing

For all things there is a purpose and for all
causes there is an effect, and where there is
smoke there is fire. Whatever and whoever
clouds your essence, cough it up, spit it out
and freely breathe.

Creating

Science offers us hi-tech tools creating brother- and sisterhoods of man on earth but the mortar of brother- and sisterhood does not come from any laboratory, it must come from the heart.

Creating

In our mysterious existence, little is truly known and all will never be experienced, and that's the challenge and fun of it. Use your creating freedom to know, experience and have fun while doing it.

Crossing

While journeying through, decide which bridge to cross, which one to burn and when to make a u-turn. Let no one drive your car with you in the driver's seat.

Crossing

When crossing the ocean in a storm,
remember staying steadfast on the ship is the
only way to cross the ocean through tears
and doubt to dry land.

Deceiving

Deceiving yourself is the easiest thing to do
but at the end of the day you have to lay
down with you in the quiet of the night.

Deciding

Do you want to live for a cause or just
because, for a purpose or no purpose, or
exist without existing, landing where you
may or any which way.

Deciding

Deciding what went wrong and why, isn't an effort or exercise in negativity but a corrective action so you can decide the best way to proceed while working smarter and not harder.

Declining

Just do it. Say no when it compromises your essence and thwarts your spirit from being productive, moving forward and being free. Saying yes to satisfy another while betraying you is a pill to disease.

Dedicating

Dedicating oneself gives purpose, meaning and gratification to an event or an outcome. Like a runner who runs every day who goes on to become an Olympic champion, like a biker cycles his way to Tour de France. Dedicate your way off poverty island onto a dreamed-of highway.

31

Defaulting

Imagining you have no faults is the greatest default.

Depending

Dependability is the greatest ability.
Everybody needs somebody at some point or some time and appreciating and embracing that truth is a soul that is free to seek and be.

Detaching

Detach from your outcome, enjoy the journey, partake the view, breathe in the morsels of fulfillment, nuggets of pleasure and seeds of joy.

Determining

In whatever position you find yourself
determine first your objective then strategize
to proceed with accuracy like an arrow
penetrating a bullseye.

Determining

Attitude determines your altitude and
gratitude determines your attitude.

Detoxing

Detox! Detox, detox, detox from all who do
not support your dreams, the associates who
possess a hidden selfish agenda, enemies
masquerading as friends, family who
degrade, toxic neighbors and backstabbing
coworkers, smiling church members who
laugh behind your back. Detox until your
passage is clear for you to drive your bus in
the direction you desire to travel and with
whom you desire to travel. Don't take any
freeloaders.

Developing

Strive hard to develop first who you are day
by day. Each day you are different, embrace
that. Don't try to be what you were
yesterday, last week or last month, wasted
energy. Never allow another to develop you
for they don't have a clue. You hold the key
to you, use it. Developing is a process and
varies day by day, year by year like
climbing a mountain you must keep trying
to reach the top.

Digressing

Digressing changes the view and
circumvents your moving forward. You
can't see what lies ahead while looking
backward. Like driving a car in reverse too
long, you are bound to get run over.

Disagreeing

Disagreeing is inevitable, learning how to agree while disagreeing is cathartic.

Discovering

Discover your passion, treat it like death and taxes, inevitable. Be unstoppable.

Discovering

Take your time discovering the beauty of the world around you, then you discover the world of beauty within you.

Dividing

Dividing happiness is like multiplying your blessings, interest on your investment with a happy return of one-hundred-fold.

Doing

Doing ordinary, ordinary you get, average
begets average but doing the extra ordinary
warrants extraordinary. Do not fall into the
average ordinary pond with get-bys and
wannabees, it's crowded.

Dreaming

D is for determination - giving it all you've
got, R is for reasons - why you want this
dream to come true, E is for enthusiasm - to
be excited about who you are, A is for ask -
ask others how to pass the test, M is for
magic - the magic of making you a winner.
Success is within your reach, as long as you
follow your DREAM.

Drinking

Always strive to drink the cup of love, peace and harmony. It makes a better you, share it with every passerby and he or she will share with another then we can all have a harmony party.

Dying

The greatest tragedy in life is not the loss of life but the greatest tragedy is a dream that is dead within as you live.

Eating

At every mental meal, eat the meat and spit out the bones. Take in all that comes across your path, select only what's required. Apply what you need, store and disregard the rest. Eating bones will disrupt, but meat will satisfy.

37

Eating

In pain, I am blessed, in my loss, I am blessed, in my heartbreak, I am blessed, in my despair, blessed, in stress, blessed. I chose to sit at my table of blessings than to lay in a tub of pain.

Eating

Some dreams do come true but in order for that to happen you have got to wake up. We cannot become what we hope to be by remaining what and where we are.

Elevating

Sometimes you may have to climb the mountain and leave some people in the valley in order to see the light.

Embarking

Before taking or embarking on a journey, chart the course to get an idea how things may turn out and let your conscience be your guide.

Empowering

Iron sharpens iron! Never stand waiting for power from someone who is not empowered to provide your need. This is personified wasted energy and dream killing. Be among others who have traveled your journey or who can identify with your chosen path and provide the helping hand pushing you up the empowerment ladder of success.

Endeavoring

Oftentimes, the future looks bleak and barren but those that endeavor will see the bleakness and barrenness disappear. Like a woman who seeks a child, no matter her age, but endeavors to make it happen and sooner or later the baby arrives because that mother endeavored it to be. Your power of endeavoring lies within, ignite it.

Enjoying

Enjoying what you have is better than plotting and planning how you're going to keep it forever. Nothing is forever not even life.

Erasing

A pencil has an eraser for a reason and a season. Erase your mistakes, grudges, pain and suffering from your psyche then start your day with a clean slate on a good foot. Now write your future legibly.

Erroring

While attempting a trial and error approach
or process, remember that most true learning
comes from the error part.

Escaping

Escaping from the old, burying yesterday,
gives a boost to the spirit. Reflex, recharge
and reboot as you escape to a better
tomorrow.

Exampling

Setting a good example speaks volumes, no
advice required as you walk the walk and
talk the talk. Everybody listens.

Exiting

Recognize when it is time to walk away
from your wilderness and drought. Seek
higher ground and not be burdened down
with a journey that is taking you nowhere
fast. Exit the desert road and drive into your
territory of milk and honey.

Expecting

Dismiss unhealthy expectations of others but
place all of your expectations on self and not
others and pray for wisdom to see the
difference. Expecting is a setup for
disappointment. Expect not to expect and
life unfolds peacefully.

Expecting

Today brings the unknown, like being pregnant you have to wait nine months for delivery. Expecting with faith in God, will unfold in due time, but don't allow your thoughts to shipwreck your course.

Experiencing

In order for someone to appreciate what you do, he or she will have to experience it. Experience is the best teacher.

Exploding

When stuck in a cave of failure and darkness find a stick of dynamite and explode your way out to freedom and daylight.

Facing

Face all obstacles. Believe you can conquer them by any means necessary one by one. Rome wasn't built in a day. Obstacles don't just fall away, you have to defeat them or they'll defeat you.

Facing

Face the music, someday you will lead the band and play your songs your way as you tinkle the ivories of your life.

Falling

Don't be afraid of falling but not getting back up. If you fall, fall on your back, if you can look up, you will get up.

Farming

Farmers farm every day, ensuring their crops will come if watered, fed and nurtured according to recipe. When the rain comes, the farmer celebrates for the crop is being watered naturally, when a storm comes he covers and protects his harvest from destruction. Life, like farming, requires preparation and action for a successful harvest, protect your harvest.

Favoring

A universal language is hearty laughter and a bright smile, do yourself a favor, do both.

Feeding

Feed your subconscious with much seed, fertilize with hope, give it to God for sunshine and rain while it germinates in your subconscious from within to without.

45

Feeling

Feelings change from moment to moment,
day to day. Don't worry it's just a feeling and
emotions are like a roller coaster, they can
run rampant without reality, so check them
at the onset. Focus on what is real and pure
and check your feelings at the door.

Flocking

Birds of a feather flock together. Maybe or
maybe not. Be aware who you flock or
labor with, you may discover you are among
sheep on a slaughtering path of destruction.

Flying

As a pilot flies a plane on automatic pilot,
give your cares to God, your automatic pilot
who has predestined your arrival and safety.

Focusing

Don't worry about what is wrong, but focus
on what is right. Right will keep you going
while wrong thwarts your focus.

Following

When intuition speaks, listen and follow. It
will never guide you wrong, go against it
and you will wish you had followed.
Intuition doesn't justify, just tells you what
to do.

Following

Follow your intuition, and you will not fail.
Follow your bliss, joy will be.

Following

Be careful who you follow, they may try to
lead you to devastation as they jump over
the hurdles.

Footprinting

Leaving your footprints on the sands of
time, you must first get up and tread
somewhere.

Forgetting

Forgetting your blessings is not an option,
but forgetting your troubles is. How
different your world would be.

Forgiving

Forgiveness is unlocking the door to set someone free and realizing you were the prisoner. You stood at the cell door with the key to your freedom but had not the insight to set yourself free. Use your forgiving key, unlock your spirit and exit your jail.

Forgiving

When a situation or person occupies your being negatively, you are a prisoner. In your hand lies the solution to freedom. Free your spirit and the rest will follow.

Forsaking

Just when I felt God had forsaken me, even though in my heart I knew He hadn't but emotions superseded, then bang there He was.

49

Forwarding

Sometimes the best way to go forward is to look backward into your history and wallow in it. Get up, shake the dust off your feet, take another route and follow your bliss to happiness.

Forwarding

Always put your best feet forward, don't just go with the flow, you may get swept away somewhere. Be your current, move with purpose and intent.

Freezing

Life is filled with successes and failures, ups
and downs, causes and effects. Freeze all
that tried to beset you, not to be thawed out
again. Everything has its place, find yours
and leave it there.

Fruiting

If you were a fruit tree, and your fruit fell to
the ground, would a passerby pick it up and
keep it or look at it and throw it back for the
birds.

Gaining

You can't gain ground, if you're standing
still, you can't move a mountain, if you
never go near it, you can't accomplish
without any effort.

Gaming

The game of life is played well by those who learn the rules, know the rules and live the rules.

Gifting

Life is a gift, a privilege of a lifetime to be who you are. God's gift to you is your talent, your gift back to God is using your talent for humanity.

Gluing

Seek all beneficial things around, attach yourself like glue, adhering with a bond that cannot be loosened without your consent.

GPS'ing

Life does have its moments that drain one's energy - spiritually, physically, financially and socially. Stop, take a moment, refuel, set your GPS in the direction you aspire and drive with no regrets and spot the potholes in advance to surpass them.

Grabbing

When the wind blows grab it until it subsides. Troubles don't last always. Grab hold with all your might, look ahead for a better sight, the rainbow is emerging.

Greasing

Like an engine needs oil, a TV needs electricity, grass needs water, the desert needs rain, your effort needs motion from stagnation. Insanity is doing the same thing and expecting different results. Rusted actions get rusted results, greased actions get greased results.

Growing

Growing pains, stretch you to the next level
of maturity. It never feels good when you're
going through it, but at the end of the tunnel,
you will leap for joy having made it through.
Roll the coaster and do not let the coaster
roll you.

Handling

When handling others reach into your heart,
when handling yourself, reach into your
head.

Harvesting

Find your harvest and glean without tiring.
Nothing good comes easy, least everyone
would have it. The harvest is plentiful but
the laborers are few. With each picking, pick
with faith and gratitude, payday is coming
after awhile. Harvest while it is day, when
night comes no one can harvest.

Heading

Heads you win, tails you lose. We have two
ends, one to sit on and one to think with.
Success comes depending on which state
you find yourself in for a period of time.

Healing

Take the opportunity to ease another's mind.
Seizing the opportunity and acting on it, is
what makes you a healer to the healed.

Helping

Help comes in all flavors and often
sometimes from unsuspecting avenues.
Always listen more than you talk and be
prepared to give more than you receive and
watch your dividends multiply. Tune in and
know there is a time to help others, there is a
time to help thyself and a time to be helped.

Helping

A helping hand is a helping hand when the receiver has a need and desire. It's wonderful to help, just use wisdom along with love. Everyone doesn't want a helping hand, know when to do it or not.

Helping

Someday everybody needs a helping hand, do your part today and a hand will appear on your day.

Hiding

Hiding who you really are should not be your job, but being truthful to yourself and others your career.

Hitchhiking

Hitchhikers walking toward a destination
will more likely be picked up than someone
who is standing in one place with a sign or
note.

Holding

Change your mindset, focus and assess who
you are and where you are, HOLD ON
because that's the fast track to greatness.

Hydrating

Hydrate yourself with all things positive and
pleasing to your soul. When your gauge is
low, refuel with positive light energy then
drive with the flow in the universe. It will
take you to the place you are supposed to be
and at the time you are supposed to arrive.

Ignoring

There is a voice inside everyone, ignore it
and you will wind up frustrated, bored and
unfulfilled. Ignoring your intuition can be
costly, paying a price you weren't prepared
to pay.

Imposing

Don't allow others to impose upon you, this
will make your spirit cringe and block your
channel of creativity.

Impressing

Be who you are and make sure your first
impression counts, for you can't recart
spilled milk.

__Improving__

Improving yourself and not your neighbor is the first step to making this world a better place for all.

__Inclining__

Incline to be free of drudgeries that may beset you. Incline to be like the birds in the air flying free, the trees in the field saluting the sun, the flowers in the garden sprouting forth, animals in the plains grazing with ease. Incline not to allow your pipes to be clogged with the dirt of life. Flush out your pipes, exhale staleness and inhale freshness.

Ingesting

Ingest love, hope, joy and peace while
infecting the universe and who crosses your
path as they ingest the beauty you behold.

Inspiring

Be the inspiration you want to see coming
from another with the innocence of a child.
Give it unconditionally. A smile for a sad
face, or comfort to the distraught. Life is a
two-way street, you inspire one way,
inspiration comes back another way. Like
money in the bank, you put it there and it
pays off after a while. What you send out, is
what you get back with interest.

Inspiring

Your gift to humanity should be to inspire in another the goodness you see in them. Sometimes we can't see ourselves, our goodness for the trees in the forest. Inspiration goes a long way, clearing the fog from loneliness, suicide, or depression. Move a tree from a forest, let the inspiration begin so what you see they will, too.

Integrating

Integrating your weakness with your strength is your totality. Embrace the real you and let no one else mold you into their likeness and for their benefits. In your totality embrace that you are enough for you. Embrace your totality while you embrace others' totality and feel how grounded your spirit becomes. Let no one know you, better than you.

Intuiting

Your intuition is your automatic pilot and will take you to your destination but you must program it where you want to go, trust that it is done and visualize your destination. Within you lies your roadmap to your desires and dreams. Embed subconscious on automatic pilot and soar.

Intuning

Being intuned, no stone is left unturned, no road is not traveled and no idea is dismissed. Nothing just happens for no reason but for a season and that season may be yours but your spirit must awaken and be intuned so that you are receptive when it appears otherwise you may miss it and it may not come again.

Jobbing

If you have no job, and get a small one and think you are too big for the small job, wake up, you are too small for a bigger job. Appreciate what you have for more.

Judging

Please do not judge the book by the cover. The person you least suspect may be the very person who may possess what you need. Never discount anyone due to their packaging. It is just a cover but underneath may lie a pot of gold just waiting to be solicited. Judge not the book by the cover, read it first.

Judging

Don't judge another for what may appear to be happening in the spur of the moment, your view may be flawed.

63

Judging

Never stand judging that which you don't
understand or have not walked in the steps
of another for a mile.

Knowing

Whatever you seek, seeks you. Faith, time
and patience are the seeds to fruition. Be
still and know.

Knowing

Know when to let go, go forth and watch
out. Be wise in all things and doings.

Knowing

You can make better choices when you have better awareness. Awareness of what you know is a step toward learning what you need to know.

Lacking

Lacking is like being in neutral and not going anywhere. If you think you lack, you will. What you think or focus on will surface. Lack is abundance turned inside out. It's a state of mind. You can achieve what your mind can achieve but you must believe and act accordingly. Don't allow lack to have free rent in your house.

Laughing

When things aren't the way you desire, laugh, until they change, when your world appears to be crumbling at your feet, find a reason to laugh, look around and behold another whose plight makes yours look like a vacation on steroids, so laugh.

<u>Laughing</u>

When you can honestly laugh at yourself
with others, you have truly made peace with
who you are and this is a sign of greatness.

<u>Leading</u>

In the rapidly changing world we live in,
unless we stand up and become leaders in
our life and in our business, we are the one
to be led and your destination may not be
desirable.

<u>Leading</u>

Being a leader is an acquired skill. Knowing
how to follow, a good leader this makes.
There is a time to lead and a time to follow.
A good leader respects and recognizes the
time of the day it is.

Leaping

Leap even when you don't know what the outcome will be but at the right time the net will appear to support you. Leap as far as you can see and when you get to a point, you will be able to see farther as you leap to higher ground.

Learning

Stick with those who have consistently pulled off the same thing you're trying to pull off. You'll learn something.

Learning

Learn to know what worked and what didn't work for others so you will become as effective as possible.

Legacying

A reputation should be like iron train tracks,
they precede and succeed, directing many
cabooses to a destination.

Letting go

Letting go of old, making room for the new
and the wisdom to do so is priceless.
Yesterdays may not be appropriate for
todays, letting go is the gateway to a current
bridge. Don't be afraid to cross it. If your
closet is filled to its capacity, you can't buy
new clothes to add until you eliminate a few.
If the shoe no longer fits, then you can't
wear it. Letting go is letting life be all that it
can be.

Listening

Sharpen your listening skills to hear inwardly. Allow your intuition to lead you to all good things outwardly.

Living

If today was your last day on Earth, what would you do, how would you live, who would you help and what would be your legacy? Can we play your tape and say "he or she lived to the fullest" or do we say "another one bites the dust unfulfilled." Food for thought. Wake up and smell the coffee, no one gets out alive. You are born to die and in between is your living .

Living

You were born to live and die! One choice you can control is how you live. Live well with purpose and intent.

Living

Living life's questions is far more rewarding than seeking life's answers. Experience is your best teacher.

Living

Live like tomorrow is not promised, and learn like you will be here for eternity. You make a life by living to its fullest.

Losing

Don't lose yourself in someone else's perception, it's only their truth and not your reality.

Losing

Most of us are born an original and die a copy. Stop trying to be someone you're not, or trying to fit into a mold that wasn't meant for you. You are unique, champion it, and know that no one can duplicate you better than you. Being a copy will sooner or later choke you alive and then you may become the walking dead inside, a misfit who has lost its way.

Losing

Sometimes a loss is a gain. All things and people are not meant to be permanent fixtures in your lives. Some come to share a lesson while others are there to support. Accepting this reality removes the sting when a friend, relative, coworker, or neighbor is no longer part of your circle. Embrace the gain, and accept the lost and prepare for the new.

71

Loving

The remedy to love is to love more and the one you should love more is you.

Lubricating

Knowing what makes you tick, like the clock maker, you chime right in when your ticker gets stuck, lubricating the part to keep on ticking.

Maturing

Obstacles that used to upset, offset and affect you are now flickers of momentary thoughts. Maturing makes this so. Being grounded makes you solid as a rock.

Maturing

Maturity doesn't always equal restraint.
Life sometimes requires acting on an
impulse then holding back.

Measuring

Measuring your progress is required so
you'll know how far you have come and
how far you need to go.

Mentoring

We all need a kind word or a friendly face
sometime, somewhere. Seek out a mentor
who will nudge, push and stretch you toward
another level, especially when you come to a
gridlock.

Mentoring

Find a mentor to follow, be a mentor to lead.
Life is a two-way street, someone helps you,
then you help another. As you walk the walk
and talk the talk, it's a win-win and a shorter
trip for all.

Minding

High achievers discuss ideas, medium
achievers discuss events, mediocre achievers
discuss people. Put your best foot forward
no regrets.

Mistaking

Realizing and understanding a mistake is a
step away from being a bit more wise.

Mixing

Mixing all that you were with all that you
are with all that you hope to be is the recipe
for your better days to come. Put all your
ingredients in the same pot, simmer and
watch as your pot overflows with the desires
of your heart.

Mothering

Find someone, anyone, lend a helping hand
who may have lost their way. Show them
the path, teach them how to walk the path,
pat them on the back and send them off with
a motherly touch with confidence, faith and
determination.

Moving

Get out of the slow lane, you may get run
over. Go with the flow until you arrive.

No'ing

You'll have to say "no" to make time for the "yes." Permit no lodging, you need the space for yourself.

Overcoming

You can only overcome your position when you know your condition. Every day presents battles and wars, choose which are worth overcoming and which are not yours to overcome.

Overcoming

Overcoming adversity takes willpower and ability. Know when the time is right to fight the battle or let it be.

Overcoming

The challenges you face will have a story of woe to tell once you are done with them and this will strengthen your resolve and others'.

Overcoming

It is easier to overcome an obstacle or situation in your physical environment than an obstacle or situation in your head. The hardest part is knowing the difference between the two.

Owing

What the world owes you is mute but what you owe the world is purposeful and destiny.

Parachuting

The mind is like a parachute, it works best
when opened. No one enters a closed door,
it must be made ajar to gain entrance. Like
energy needs to flow, your mind needs to be
open to experience.

Patterning

Patterning and moving in the direction of
those you admire and trust, illuminates your
every step while treading in their footsteps.

Permitting

Yesterday is gone, today is here and
tomorrow is not promised. Let nothing or
no one turn you around without your
permission.

Phoning
Phoning is a communicable asset that
permits a channel to seek what seeks you.
No one is an island, everyone has something
another needs but you must phone in to get
it. Cry out to the universe with sincerity and
it will answer back with commitment.

Pianoing
Life can be like playing the piano. The more
you play the better you get. Practice,
practice makes perfect and perfect makes
perfection.

Planning
Always start with a plan, when Plan A
falters don't despair, apply Plan B and if
Plan B fails, no worries because there are
twenty-three more alphabets for you to get it
right.

79

Planning

Failing to plan, is a sure roadmap to
planning to fail. Not knowing which way to
go, you may wind up nowhere.

Playing

Don't worry about getting on base first, just
make sure you stay in the game and play
your position.

Pleasing

You can't please all the people all the time
so don't worry about pleasing them anytime,
just be true to yourself and let the rest be
history.

Plucking

It is not a shame to pluck away friends or
family who stand in your way of happiness
because they want to. Like weeds in your
garden choking your plants to death. It's not
a shame to do so, but a shame not to.

Positioning

Position yourself among others that can
assist in making your dream a reality.
Dismiss all little No's and receive the big
YES. When one door closes another will
open, see it and stride through.

Positioning

Location, location. Position yourself among the greats whose paths you desire to tread. Carefully chart their steps, then order your steps climbing to your mountaintop. You may slow up but don't stop, you may tire, rest but continue, you may despair, begin anew. In the blink of an eye, you will arrive.

Positioning

When life beats you down and you fall to your knees, stay there, it's a good position to send up a prayer.

Possessing

When you are rich in admiration and gratitude, free from envy, enjoying the greatness of others, loving generously, unconditionally and sharing selflessly, you are in possession of gifts money cannot buy.

82

Possessing

From birth you possess the right to be you,
don't allow nothing or no one to take that
right away without your permission.

Practicing

Practicing takes time and effort but the
rewards money can't buy. Jackie Robinson,
like Muhammad Ali, didn't will themselves
to greatness but practicing made it so.
Practice makes perfect while you perfect
your legacy in history. Doing makes it so.

Praising

Praising is worshiping as you set your soul
assail to bond with a higher source, God,
nature, oneness. Like going back home and
being welcomed back into the fold.

Praying

If you're going to pray don't worry, if you are going to worry don't pray. With prayer release it to God, leave it at his feet and don't pick it back up. Trust that all is well and will be for your betterment. To God be the glory.

Praying

Praying is a two-way street. One street to send and another to receive what will be sent. If there are roadblocks on either paths, you communication may be limited. Remove the debris from your path, get out of your way and then pray.

Preaching

There are days that will require you to preach and there are days that will require you to be preached to. Know what time it is. When you are feeling unheard, unseen, unfulfilled, get preached to. To help another in need, preach.

Preparing

Preparation, determination and faith feeds into success like a duck takes to water and a bird flies in the air.

Presenting

Present your product, You, in the kind of light that will make you shine even in the midst of darkness.

Previewing

Some decisions don't come with a preview
of highlights. Know today you may have to
pay the admission to see the show.

Pricing

Know your worth, otherwise someone may
put a cheaper price, sale price on you.

Proceeding

It is better to have expectations and strive
toward them than to have doubts and spiral
down to them.

Processing

Like technology when life crashes all around
you and there is nothing left to do, get some
new software and move on to a new day and
a new way while processing the failures not
to repeat again.

Processing

Life if filled with daily processing of the
happenings, good and bad, to teach one how
to live a purposeful life.

Procrastinating

Procrastination is the thief of dreams, goals,
time and eventually your life.
Procrastination is a bridge to regret street
and despair road.

Promising

Under-promise and over deliver, at the end
of the day you have a satisfied customer,
You.

Promoting

It is your own responsibility to take charge
of your own success. Go out and promote
your existence. Businesses don't succeed in
the first year because of lack of promotion.

Promoting

When in a privileged position, promote good
will while creating desirable solutions to
common problems for uncommon
opportunities.

Protecting

Protecting your heart with all diligence is a must. Once broken, it will never be the same. Like a parade, if you don't want someone to rain on your parade, don't tell them where you're parading.

Providing

A new day won't do anything for you except provide the time for which you can do something different for yourself or another.

Pulling

Inspiration and passion keep you going, your faith in God is your pulling life line.

Putting

Today put your best feet forward, don't just go with the flow, you may get swept away to an undesirable place.

Questioning

Questioning yourself is crucial, living the answers is life.

Quieting

Quieting the noise in your head, allows your inner soundtrack to play. Be still and focus with your third eye as you receive all that you seek to know for it seeks you to know it.

Reaching

Reaching will stretch you in new dimensions, just make sure you stretch far enough to help another and not just yourself.

Reaching

Reach for the mountaintop, if you don't get there expeditiously, it will stretch you to get there eventually.

Reacting

Reacting to life is ten percent of what happens to you and how you respond is ninety percent.

91

Readying

The more ready you are for challenge,
obstacles and disappointments, the less
competitive towards others you will feel
because you are truly focused on your
journey.

Realizing

Disappointment is inevitable,
discouragement is a choice and expectation
is a trap. Be your own judge and jury.

Receiving

Receiving what is given is a blessing, taking
without agreement is a horse of another
color.

Reflecting

Reflecting on where you have been, where you are and where you hope to be in the future, opens the mental door to chart a path worth taking the journey for you to know from whence you came and have a plan to go where you need to be.

Reframing

You are the picture in your life, reframe it anytime you want to, anyway you desire and anyhow you deem. Enjoy the view, you created it.

Reinventing

Yesterday you were, today you are and tomorrow you should be. Take stock of the market, see what's current, adapt and overcome. Outdatedness gets you leftovers from yesterday.

93

Rekindling

Rekindling is an attribute that keeps you from going down when all else appears to be going down like the titanic. Rekindle your faith with fire to remain afloat of disturbing turbulence.

Releasing

Life is action and passion. If you have not found that one thing that wakes you up in the morning, keeps you up late at night, drives you throughout the day, and fills an area within you, passion has left the building. Invite it back in and groove to your beat.

Releasing

In life you pick up ineffective habits from well-intentioned people but true maturity allows you to replace these with effective habits thereby freeing the incarcerated you.

94

Remaining

Remaining on a road that is clearly not
leading you in the direction you want to go
makes no sense like sitting in the back seat
of a car and expecting it to drive you to your
destination.

Remembering

Remember pain can only deter you when
you allow, like joy will only emerge once
permitted.

Remembering

Niceties are important and should not be
skipped. Do the things that spark the most
interest first and you will be remembered
fondly.

<u>Removing</u>

Remove the old blooms from your flowers, so new blooms can appear, purge dead people from your space, so live ones will appear like sunlight beaming on a bright day.

<u>Repeating</u>

The beginning of a habit is like an invisible thread, but every time you repeat it you strengthen the strand until it becomes a great cable that holds you up when you need the lift and support.

<u>Replacing</u>

The new replaces the old, while the present replaces the past and the future becomes a new present so accept it, be grateful and use it strategically.

Replaying

If you keep doing the same thing over and over again with the same result than it's time to change the record for a new tune.

Respecting

Little 'u's and big 'I's cannot happily coexist in the same space until the realization that labels divide and suppress while respecting joins and support.

Resting

You cannot tell how good the day has been until night has come. Make it a good day, no regrets and you will rest peacefully.

Resulting

When you're not selling, you're being out sold, when you're not networking, you're not working.

Retiring

Retiring old endings is just a new day for new beginnings to do what you sought to do yesterday but couldn't.

Revenging

Revenge may be sweet but its fruit is bitter leaving a sting even in the heart of the revenger and the revengee.

<u>Reviving</u>

Seek moments when you can revive another
with a breath of fresh air. They breathe, you
breathe, it's all the same air.

<u>Rewarding</u>

Rewarding yourself for all of your
accomplishments, it's like paying yourself
first. If you don't champion yourself first,
then who?

<u>Rewarding</u>

Rewarding the universe by sending out
positive energy to all you encounter is
rewarding your spirit with delight.

Rewriting

Your reality, may not be truth. Detach if necessary. Rewrite your program, if it's not working.

Ridding

Get rid of all the rats in your life, they only want to eat what you have and destroy your house.

Rising

Rise up to your situation or your situation will rise above you. Rise with action and purpose to defeat or your situation defeats you.

Rising

Rising to the top, you must remember how it feels to be at the bottom. The view is different.

Roping

Your neighbor appears to be drowning, throw in your rope, you may need them at some point to throw the rope back to you. Do unto others.

Saluting

Saluting the beauty in others, permits others to salute the beauty within you. Saluting sends out energy and it goes back and forth igniting all in its path.

101

Savoring

Savoring the good times will hold you up
when the bad times tries to beat you down.

Searching

Only someone who knows where you come
from can take you where you're going.

Seeding

When seeding be careful where you plant.
On stony ground, your seeds will be choked
but on fertile ground, your seed will sprout
forth with the rising sun.

Seeing

Seeing God's hand in everything and
everywhere, you can sit back in your easy
chair and allow all to unfold.

Seeking

At the end of the day, will life find you
climbing up a new mountain or sliding down
an old mountain?

Seeking

Books, newspapers, events, and social media
are seeking you with answers toward your
destiny but you must open the book, read the
newspaper, attend the event and utilize the
internet to discover your gifts.

Seeking

Seeking with your spiritual eye, you see
what so many others can't begin to see. Who
knows you may be an old soul.

Self-sufficient

Being self-sufficient is fulfilling to your soul
like having gas in your car, you are ready to
go.

Self Teaching

Self teaching like experience is the best
teacher. Learn like you are going to live
forever. Be a sponge soaking up all that
crosses your path, wring out what you don't
need and store the rest.

104

Selling

When you are selling a product, it first begins with you. And for God's sake don't sell yourself without a smile on your face, no one wants to buy from a stone.

Sending

Sending prayers of peace to someone who has wronged you deeply like a family member or friend or a boss and not feel any negative feelings or anger or pain in your gut but a calmness of spirit is true forgiveness while you send them peace and prayers. Sending is rewarding.

Sharpening

Take time to sharpen your sixth sense, when
you need it it will cut through the chase for
you like a double-edged sword.

Sitting

Sitting by the water waiting for a bite, you
got to put bait on the hook to catch the fish.

Sizing

What counts most is not the size of the dog
in the fight but it's the size of the fight in the
dog.

Skipping

Skipping over mistakes that befell others,
makes your life one mistake less. Learn
from others, you won't live long enough to
make all the mistakes of life and shouldn't
want to.

Smiling

Smiles, everyone's got one. Some are
hidden and some are not but one thing for
sure a smile's price never increases nor does
its value decrease.

Soaring

Soaring keeps you moving and not standing
still. Stagnant gets stagnant results.
Insanity is doing the same thing and
expecting different results. Soar like an
eagle, eliminate geese, they hold you back.

Sowing

Sow good seeds, it may take a minute but be assured, your harvest will come!

Squeezing

You can only get lemon juice when you squeeze the lemon. Squeezing will make the real you come out and challenges are the tools to make that happen.

Standing

Standing in the face of adversity, teaches endurance and builds character in your core. Lean or bend but keep standing for this too has a life span.

Standing

Standing firm with your DNA's blueprint
does not have to be validated by another's
ignorance. Stand for who you are, otherwise
you'll fall for anything that comes across
your path.

Starting

Starting doesn't have to start with knowing
all there is to know, every 'T' doesn't have
to be crossed and every 'I' doesn't have to
be dotted. It's like a puzzle, piece by piece,
eventually you will see the picture that is
before you.

Staying

Staying in a comfortable bed is like
wallowing in your bad habits, easy to get
into and hard to get out of.

109

Stepping

Stepping passed all the no's that are thrown
your way is just a stepping stone to the yes
that awaits your footprint.

Stopping

Recognize and stop doing permanent things
with temporary people.

Strengthening

Strengthening often comes from obstacles
and remains long enough to allow you to
realize they exist. Learning the lesson to
avoid repeating it.

Stressing

Stressing circumvents your energy and distorts your view making the possible impossible. You become like a car without an engine, you try and try but go nowhere.

Striking

When opportunity knocks you must open the door for it may never come again. Strike the coal while it is hot and you will benefit but if you wait until it is cold, the work is twice as hard. You don't put out your umbrella once the rain has ended.

Striving

Striving requires doing even when the doing is tough and you don't feel like it. Strive with those who are going in your direction, they can teach you a thing or two.

111

Stuffing

If there is a turkey in your midst today,
identify it, stuff it and move on. You can't
soar like an eagle with turkeys on your back.

Submitting

Submitting your needs into the universe,
will allow the universe to return it back to
you. What goes up, comes down, what goes
out, comes back.

Suffering

Suffering in silence speaks so loud
everybody is listening and knows your
game.

Sweating

Sweating is like opening your spirit to release the toxins and to receive the oxygen of life to propel your soul clean.

Taking

Never take a NO from someone who is not empowered to give you a YES. And never take a shirt from a naked person.

Talking

Talking while listening, no can do. Find the time to do one or the other. You have two ears and one mouth so listen more than you talk. Each has its time and place. To do or not to do, discover when.

113

Taping

At the end of your life when all is said and done do we play your tape or wish we hadn't?

Tasking

When called by God to do a task, don't worry about how or who's watching over your shoulder. It's your task.

Telephoning

Prayer is you telephoning God, intuition is God guiding and directing you and sharing is you giving back to God.

Thanking

Thanking with gratitude is knowing you had nothing to do with an outcome of a thing hoped for but was granted because of mercy and grace.

Thanking

Thanking is focusing on all that is right and not on what is wrong while being grateful that it isn't worse, for you could be the jobless, homeless, sick and hopeless.

Thinking

Thinking your problem is huge makes it so. If you think you can, you will, if you think you can't you won't. If you think better is possible, then think good is not enough.

Thinking

Thoughts drive actions. Make sure yours are the right ones. Once released they are what they are. Guard your thoughts with all diligence for they are like propellers.

Throwing

Throwing dirt at someone, be careful the wind may blow the dirt back in your face.

Timing

God sends people in our lives at the perfect time with the perfect solutions. Be aware not to overlook your perfect solution from a perfect source while focusing in the wrong direction.

Timing

Time is on your side once you come in
agreement with it and proceed accordingly.
Racing against time is a futile effort that
leads to exhaustion. Agree and be.

Tolerating

Tolerating the bad may get you to the good,
the bitter to get to the sweet, the ugly to
beauty. It's a mighty long road that never
ends and a mighty long wind that never
changes. Good things come to those who
tolerate and celebrate.

Topping

Stay on top of your intentions or they may topple you. Write them down, avoid losing them in the shuffle.

Tracking

Be like a tracker leaving your tracks in the sand for others to follow as you role model being an altruist. Why reinvent the wheel, when you can take the one available and move forward at a greater pace. Seek the tracks or wheels you need and proceed.

Trailing

Trailing in the footsteps of a forerunner, staying your course, going forward don't look back unless the footsteps take you back.

Traveling

Knowing which way to go is good, but how you will get there is crucial.

Treating

Be careful how you treat people on your way up, the tide may turn and you just may have to greet those same people on your way down.

Trusting

When God leads you to the edge of the cliff, trust Him fully and let go, only one or two things will happen, either God will catch you when you fall or He will teach you how to fly.

Trusting

Relationships are nurtured and don't happen overnight, trusting that you are in the right one is intuitive.

Trusting

Trusting that you have all the resources you need to accomplish, and if it is to be it will be and if it doesn't happen then it wasn't meant to be especially if you did all you could, fret not, if tomorrow comes you can begin anew. Treat your valleys as mere stepping stones to your mountain.

Trying

There is no failure in trying, but the real failure is in not trying. Trying comes in cans and not cannots.

Turning

Realizing life has gotten off track, don't wait
for a turning point, grab the steering wheel
and turn with all your power.

Turtling

Being a turtle is okay, just keep moving as
you stick your head out to see your way
clear to your destination.

Turtling

Turtling your way through when hard times
hit, creep along, this will surely pass.
Nothing remains the same forever.

Understanding

To understand how things truly are, you must eliminate and strip away some of the erroneous information you've been taught and start over.

Unearthing

Unearth the gem that lies beneath your surface with meditation, chanting and prayer. Think you've got it, you will search, think you haven't got it, you won't search.

Unlocking

Try every key you can find to unlock your passion from bondage. Like an Easter egg hunt, you turn over every stone or rock to find your egg. Unlocking your passion allows you to live with purpose for a purpose.

Unthawing

Unthaw from the depths of sorrow and
regret, you can't see your future while
gazing at your past.

Unwavering

When your gut feeling tells you to go forth,
strive unwaveringly to make the intangible,
tangible, the unforeseen seen. Unwaver and
you fail not.

U-turning

U-turning is required when you see the
roadblock up ahead. Don't wait for the ship
to go down before you jump off. Do all you
can, stand when you can, and u-turn when
you must.

Viewing

Try to see the light side of things, it's the
dark side that everyone views. The glass is
half full.

Visioning

See your vision and make it plain. Without a
vision, you dry up like a raisin left in the
sun, become the walking dead and blind
while you don't see.

Visualizing

See things not as they are but as you desire
them to be by feeding your subconscious to
attract what it knows. You reap what you
sow. You can't sow apples and expect
oranges.

Volunteering
Volunteering is your greatest gift to
humankind, an asset that speaks volume.

Waiting
Waiting is a virtue, while wandering through
your wilderness. In due season, your guiding
rainbow will appear.

Waiting
Don't wait for another to come along and
give you a helping hand. You have two
hands, use them wisely. One to push you
and the other to lift you up. Don't wait for a
ride when the bus is going your way.

Waiting

Why wait for tomorrow, you know damn
well it's not promised. Don't fool yourself,
you have to lay down with you.

Wanting

Wanting doesn't get you anywhere. Wanting
to be successful without action is like
dreaming and never waking up. Wanting to
exercise doesn't help you lose weight.
Wanting to quit smoking doesn't stop you
from smoking. Wanting to stop overeating
doesn't close your mouth.

Wasting

Every day is the beginning of the rest of your life, don't waste it. Have no regrets and please don't allow woulda, coulda, shoulda to hang on your lips. Tomorrow is not promised, yesterday is gone and today is the present. Receive it with appreciation, go forth. Waste not, want not.

Wasting

Don't waste your thoughts and efforts on useless distractions for at the end of the day, it won't matter anyway. Choose your battles and know that the war is already won because God says so and nothing else matters.

127

Wasting

Don't waste your energy on the energyless,
or hope on the hopeless or giving to a taker.
Drain in drain out.

Watching

Watching the clock doesn't change your
future, but wastes your present.

Wedding

With this ring I pledge to love myself
unconditionally by accepting all my faults
and flaws, this day forward I will be me and
no one else and will allow others to be free
to be.

128

Wheelbarrowing

Be not like a wheelbarrow only going where
pushed, sitting where placed and dumping
when dumped.

Whining

When feeling the need to whine, think again,
nobody wants to hear it.

Winning

Winning is not the prize but the journey to
winning is the prize. Enjoy the trip.

Wondering

Wondering if you could be, will never make
it so, just leaves you wondering what
happened to you.

Working

Working with ethics and integrity, will open
quality doors that you are ready to step into.

Worrying

Stop worrying about what you will be
tomorrow and know that you are somebody
today and that's a fact.

Writing

To thine own self be true. Strive not to write a verbal check, that your butt can't cash, for you put both feet in your mouth.

Yawning

Yawning, breathing out the toxins of yesterday, inhaling the nutrients of today and rejuvenating for a better life.

Yelling

Yelling for attention may attract the wrong element, know your intent then proceed.

Yielding

Yielding to temptation is not a bad thing but what you're yielding to.

About The Author

E.P. McKnight is a native of Moss Point, Mississippi. She attended Fordham University of Lincoln Center, New York City, where she obtained her M.Ed.

As an actress, writer, poet, producer, teacher, playwright, talk show host, motivational speaker, and fitness instructor, she has spent countless hours writing inspirational and educational books and plays, aka edutainment.

McKnight is a member of SAG, and AEA and has performed globally in theatre, films, television, soap operas and commercials. She is a member of Toastmasters International.

Recent Credits: "The Trial of Scottsboro Alabama," "Catch The Spirit," "With Grace I Stand," "I Question America," "On My Own Terms," "MenApause."

See www.epmcknight.com.

Joy 365

Do not acquire someone to come in to "save the day" who was not there when "the day" did not need saving. That person does not understand "the day" the same way you do.

Sometimes you may have to open your eyes to see, and other times you may have to close them. Realize what you cannot see with your eyeballs, you will sense with your heart.

Joy365 will provide inspiration and motivation every time she sends her thoughts into the universe. She challenges us to live life to the fullest with gusto and zest! Thank you for your words that help guide us and add light to our chosen paths. *Pamela Brogdon-Wynne, Ed.D. Director, College of the Canyons*

EPMcKnight is an extraordinary, gifted and talented writer that translates life's situation into poetry. Her writing is inspiring, uplifting, comical, even sometimes emotional, causing one to pause. *Geraldine 'Lady G' Montgomery, Entrepreneur & Real Estate Investor*

EPMcKnight's books are so refreshing! They are full of inspiration that give the reader fresh new energy and determination to strive for their goals and dreams!!! *Charles Goldsmith, National Sales Director, Primerica*

We celebrate E. P. McKnight's newest writing Joy 365. Her writings always provide inspiration, motivation and heartfelt reading supported by a top-notch determination of strong perseverance to delight the visual and auditory senses. Her words read like sweet strings of musical notes to the heart to be shared by generations.
Peter and Elizabeth Dortch, Retired Educators
Educational Advocate for Christian and Academic Resources

www.ingramcontent.com/pod-product-compliance
Lightning Source LLC
Chambersburg PA
CBHW071003040426
42443CB00007B/643